Preparing for
THE
COMING
REVIVAL

How to Lead a Successful Fasting & Prayer Gathering

Bill Bright

New Life
PUBLICATIONS
A MINISTRY OF CAMPUS CRUSADE FOR CHRIST

Preparing for the Coming Revival

Published by
NewLife Publications
A ministry of Campus Crusade for Christ
100 Sunport Lane
Orlando, FL 32809

Design and typesetting by Genesis Publications.

Printed in the United States of America.

ISBN 1-56399-075-X

Unless otherwise indicated, Scripture quotations are from the *New International Version*, ©1973, 1978, 1984 by the International Bible Society. Published by Zondervan Bible Publishers, Grand Rapids, Michigan.

Scripture quotations designated TLB are from *The Living Bible*, ©1971 by Tyndale House Publishers, Wheaton, Illinois.

For more information, write:
Life Ministries—P.O. Box 40, Flemington Markets, N5W 2129, Australia
Campus Crusade for Christ of Canada—Box 300, Vancouver, B.C., V6C 2X3, Canada
Campus Crusade for Christ—Fairgate House, King's Road, Tyseley, Birmingham, B11 2AA, England
Campus Crusade for Christ—P.O. Box 8786, Auckland, New Zealand
Campus Crusade for Christ—Alexandra, P.O. Box 0205, Singapore 9115, Singapore
Great Commission Movement of Nigeria—P.O. Box 500, Jos, Plateau State Nigeria, West Africa
Campus Crusade for Christ International—100 Sunport Lane, Orlando, FL 32809, USA

As a personal policy, Bill Bright has never accepted honorariums for speaking or royalties for his personal use. Any royalties from this book or the more than fifty other books by Bill Bright are dedicated to the glory of God and designated to promoting spiritual revival through discipleship training and evangelism around the world.

Contents

Acknowledgments

My special thanks go to Nancy Leigh DeMoss and Dr. Henry Blackaby for their inspiration and enthusiasm for spiritual awakening and revival and the fulfillment of the Great Commission. This leader's manual has been a team effort. I want to thank Dr. Steve Clinton, president of the Orlando Institute, a Campus Crusade for Christ university in Orlando, Florida; the NewLife Publications staff: Don Tanner, director of publishing; Joette Whims; and Lynn Copeland of Genesis Publications who spent many hours helping me prepare and edit this manuscript.

A Personal Word

For more than fifty years, I have prayed for revival for our nation and its people. As I travel tens of thousands of miles throughout our beautiful land each year speaking in many churches, on campuses, and to business and professional groups, I have seen the devastation and misery that people everywhere are facing because we have abandoned our godly heritage.

Tragically, we as a nation are disobeying and grieving God. I think primarily of the colossal insult to our God and heavenly Father when we betrayed Him and the trust of our Founding Fathers by removing prayer and Bibles from our schools. The basis for our moral and spiritual integrity as a nation is gone. As a result, an avalanche of evil, crime, immorality, abortion, alcohol and drug addiction has devastated our country and broken the heart of our Lord. Homes are divided, corruption has sprung up in many places, and dishonesty and greed have destroyed lives. Like ancient Israel, our nation has officially forgotten God and failed to obey His commands (Deuteronomy chapters 8 and 28).

That's why I was so thrilled when God began moving in a new and wonderful way in my life and in the lives of others. For me, it started July 5, 1994, when God led me to begin a forty-day fast during which I asked God to send a great spiritual awakening to our nation and the world and for the fulfillment of the Great Commission. On my twenty-ninth day of fasting, I was reading in 2 Chronicles, chapters 28 through 30, when God's holy Word spoke to my heart in a most unusual way. I felt impressed by the Lord to invite several hundred of the most influential Christians in the country to gather in Orlando, Florida, December 5–7, 1994, as guests of Campus Crusade for a time of fasting and prayer. This would be strictly a time for seeking God's direction on how we, His servants, can be channels of revival for our nation and the world and for the fulfillment of the Great Commission.

My staff and I prayed for at least a Gideon's three hundred to respond. Instead, more than six hundred Christian leaders, representing more than a hundred denominations and religious organizations, gathered for the event. And God met with us in a supernatural way. Many remarked how they had never been a part of anything so spiritually powerful in their lives.

The overwhelming response to the initial gathering prompted us to schedule an even larger conference, called Fasting and Prayer '95, in Los Angeles in November 1995. I doubt that we will ever fully comprehend the magnitude of what God will do as a result of these fasting and prayer gatherings. But we have every reason to believe that His plan includes a mighty revival from heaven.

In writing this leadership manual, I want to be very careful that I am not misunderstood. Fasting does not make one a member of the spiritually elite. The Pharisees made fasting and prayer a point of ritual and boasting to demonstrate their piety (Matthew 6:16–18), and Jesus rebuked them for their attitude. Instead, true fasting creates in us a sense of humility. If we fast with a pure heart, the very thought of exalting ourselves will be abhorrent. However, I believe Christians should have the freedom to fast openly. How else can they be mentors of this spiritual discipline to others, promote fasting on a large scale, or participate in a church-wide fasting and prayer gathering? (See my book *The Coming Revival*, pages 147–149, for a complete discussion of this topic.) My desire is to encourage believers to fast and pray together in large numbers in their churches so they will be an inspiration to others.

I want to be cautious that I do not sound like I am beating a *fasting* drum. *I am committed to evangelism and discipleship.* I try to evaluate everything I do every day in light of the Great Commission. Through the years, God has graciously enabled my associates and me to help train millions of Christians in discipleship and evangelism in most countries of the world. However, I sincerely believe that this greater emphasis on the discipline of fasting with prayer will enable us all to be much more fruitful for our Lord than we have ever been.

I invite you to join me in praying that God will continue to use the fasting and prayer gatherings as a spark to help set ablaze the Body of Christ and send revival in this critical moment of history for our beloved nation and for the Church. I urge you to join others who have committed themselves to fasting and prayer and to teaching these disciplines to other Christians, inspiring believers to trust our sovereign God to send revival to our needy nation and world.

Bill Bright

Preparing for Revival

Purpose: To prepare Christians to plan and conduct a gathering on fasting and prayer in a small group or a church-wide or community gathering on revival

Materials: *7 Basic Steps to Successful Fasting and Prayer*
The Coming Revival
Have You Discovered the Wonderful Adventure of the
Spirit-Filled Life?
How You Can Pray With Confidence

Instructions for this section: Obtain the resources listed above. They will give you the basic spiritual and factual foundation helpful for leading a successful fasting and prayer gathering. The materials may be obtained through your local Christian bookstore, mail-order catalog distributor, or NewLife Publications. (See the order information at the back of this manual.)

Read through these resources carefully and begin to apply the principles you learn to prepare your heart and attitude. Then study "Keep Your Flame Burning Brightly" to review the reasons why revival is essential and acquaint yourself with the steps to conducting a successful fasting and prayer gathering.

Keep Your Flame Burning Brightly

Who is responsible for revival? God or man? Do you work up a revival or do you pray one down? What can one person do to prepare for revival?

Our great and holy, righteous, and loving Creator God is sovereign. He rules in the affairs of men and nations. Everything in creation is under His control. But He has chosen to give His children the privilege of working together with Him to take the Good News of His love and forgiveness in Christ to the world. Likewise, He has entrusted to His children a vitally important role in preparing the way for revival.

Our Lord looks upon His Church, His body of believers, as the "salt of the earth" (Matthew 5:13). Salt is a necessary supplement in the human diet. It adds flavor to the food, and as a preservative, it prolongs the life of perishable items. But most Christians today have lost their savor. As many of the biblical values that Americans have held dear slowly slip away, the Church often seems powerless to preserve them.

Please do not misunderstand me. I love the church. I became a Christian through the influence of my mother's prayers and the First Presbyterian Church of Hollywood. In my almost fifty years of walking with the Lord, I have been committed to the local church. At Campus Crusade for Christ, we have a policy that every staff person must be active in a local church.

In fact, the church is the most important institution in our nation apart from the family. Each one of us is a member of Christ's Body, the Church. We all share in the hurts, disappointments, and trials of the Church in our country, and in how the local church fares in the community.

When I point out the weaknesses of the Church, it is because honest criticism is the first step toward healing and revival. As the Church of our Lord Jesus Christ goes, so goes the nation. It is therefore extremely important—life and death for our country—that the church be awakened, revived, cleansed, and made whole—or we have no hope for our nation. If we continue with the status quo, our children's children will live in a godless, immoral, degenerate Sodom and Gomorrah. Our only prospect as a nation is a spiritual revival in the Church. Remember God's words to King Solomon: "If my people"—and that includes the Church in today's world—"who are called by my name, will humble themselves and pray and seek my face and turn from their wicked ways, then will I hear from heaven and will forgive their sin and will heal their land" (2 Chronicles 7:14).

The State of the Church in Our Nation

You may be asking: Why does the Church need revival? Isn't the Holy Spirit already at work in our midst? Have we not sent out tens of thousands of missionaries to all parts of the world?

Sadly, the Church has left its first love. According to many polls and surveys, the majority of believers acknowledge that they have lost their original spiritual fervor and are caught up in the things of the world. Like the church of Ephesus (Revelation 2:1–7), they do not love the Lord as they once did. Consequently, the Church, for the most part, is sorely divided. Instead of being havens of rest for the spiritually weary, often churches are battle zones for the spiritually carnal. God is not pleased with division within His family, and He wants to unite us into one body.

In addition, the Church often reflects a poor image. Are not Christians supposed to be "salt and light"? If so, where is their mighty Christian influence in our morally bankrupt society? Salt brings flavor to food and helps preserve perishable goods. Jesus says, "If you lose your flavor, what will happen to the world?" (Matthew 5:13, TLB). Many Christians have lost their savor and are leaving a bad taste in the mouth of society. Most believers are struggling even to survive in the world, let alone preserve it.

Christians are also searching for easy solutions and quick success. It is as though the Word of God and the Spirit of God are not sufficient to cope with the problems of the '90s. So, many have turned to psychology, emphasizing the inward search, the psyche, the soul, looking for help in self-diagnosis (with a few Christian principles thrown in by writers to qualify it as Christian material).

When confronted with world conditions and the call to Christian action, many Christians reply with a shrug, "Jesus said it was going to get worse, so why worry about it?" Instead of becoming more motivated to help spread the gospel and share their faith with everyone who will listen, they live for the "rapture," for escape. They plunge themselves into pleasure-seeking and self-worship, waiting for the end to come.

Our Alternative

In talking with many prominent Christian leaders across our land, I have witnessed a growing concern for the tragic condition of America and the Church. It is obvious that the Holy Spirit has been at work among those who still listen to His voice, and in advance of the coming revival, He is creating this concern in the minds and hearts of His people. This was dramatically demonstrated by the enthusiastic response from the more than six hundred Christian leaders who attended our fasting and prayer gathering in Orlando.

These leaders will readily admit that most of the Church in America finds itself in this present state of spiritual impotence because it does not truly love God, nor trust His promises and obey

His commands. Most believers do not spend time with the Lord in prayer or study His holy Word. They do not know or appreciate His many attributes. They live with a limited view of our great Creator God, our holy heavenly Father, and our risen, incomparable, peerless Savior, the Lord Jesus Christ.

Yet each one of us has the Word of God. God has given us the ability to read, understand, and obey it. Each believer in Jesus Christ is indwelt by the Holy Spirit. We can turn to God. We can seek Him. We do not have to wait on others to lead the way. We can walk in His Spirit; we can win the struggle with our worldly nature by refusing to obey it (Galatians 5:16,17). We do not *have* to follow the ways of the world (1 Corinthians 10:13; 1 John 2:1–6; 5:4,5).

All we really have to do as believers, from the time we get up in the morning until we go to bed at night, is love God with all of our heart and soul and mind and strength, obey His commands, and trust His promises. Everything else in ministry and life flows from that relationship with Him. From the obedience of His followers, God can then move in our midst in a mighty way.

How the Revival Will Come

Revival comes as a sovereign act of God—as the result of Christian people meeting God's conditions by responding to the Holy Spirit. Revival is an answer to sincere, prevailing prayer in which God:

- Grips His people with deep conviction, repentance, forgiveness, and deliverance from personal sins
- Fills His people with the Holy Spirit and manifests in them the fruit and graces of the Holy Spirit
- Fills the Church and community with His presence and power
- Ignites in His people, young and old, a passion to bring the lost to Christ at home and around the world
- Causes non-Christians to earnestly seek Him

I believe three things must happen before local and national revival can take place:

1. *Christian leaders must catch the vision.* They must play a prominent role in presenting the call of the Holy Spirit to their congregations. I believe it is the duty of pastors to lead their people to repentance—by personal example as well as by proclamation. Other Christian leaders must also champion the call to revival.

Broadcasters, heads of parachurch organizations, evangelists, and influential lay leaders must all herald God's call to revival.

2. *God's people must heed the call to repentance, fasting, and prayer.* Before God will lift His present hand of judgment from America, believers by the millions must first humble themselves and seek His face in fasting and prayer, according to 2 Chronicles 7:14. Since fasting is a biblical means of humbling ourselves (Joel 2:12,13), it is the only spiritual discipline that enables us to meet all the conditions of this passage. God will send an awakening to this nation as His people, one by one, obey His call and yield themselves in repentance to the Spirit of God. A "broken and contrite heart" (Psalm 51:17) will always find favor with God.

3. *The Holy Spirit must convict the nation of its sins.* No revival is possible without the convicting power of the Holy Spirit (John 16:8). As Christians humble themselves before the Lord, the Holy Spirit will convict people of their sins, cause them to repent, bring healing to His people, and restore blessing to our land.

God is raising up many fasting and prayer gatherings in unprecedented numbers to prepare His people for the coming revival. I invite you to join the thousands of other leaders just like you who are calling God's people to faithfulness and holiness and to help fulfill the Great Commission.

Steps to Revival

Following are three steps to planning and holding a study on fasting and prayer in a small group or a church-wide or community gathering on revival:

1. *Make sure that you understand and are practicing the principles of fasting and prayer* given in this manual.

    ■ Review the booklet *7 Basic Steps to Successful Fasting and Prayer,* and apply the steps to your life.

    ■ Study the material in this guide to help you plan your next step.

2. *Select a group of godly men and women* who will help you prepare and conduct the gathering.

    ■ Begin with your Bible study group or the leadership in your church. If you are using this material with a small group, you may want to present all the material yourself. If you have a larger group in mind, the leadership planning section gives suggestions on how to delegate the responsibilities to others on your leadership team.

- Schedule at least one study meeting with your team to help them learn and apply the fasting and prayer principles in their lives.
- Then begin planning your event. Section 2, "Preparing Your Leadership," gives helpful material for you and your planning team, including outlines for two seminars and a prayer coordinator's guide to help you conduct effective prayer sessions during the gathering.

3. *Plan and conduct your gathering.*

- Refer to Section 3, "Conducting Your Fasting and Prayer Gathering," which provides a sample schedule and information on how to conduct your event.
- Set up prayer concerts for your meetings.
- Select the date.
- Order the needed materials for your gathering.
- Conduct the sessions and seminars and watch God work through you and your leadership team. The results will amaze you!
- Spread the flame beyond your circle of influence. Once you have held your first event, I encourage you to consider branching out with a larger fasting and prayer meeting in your community or denomination and encourage others to do the same.

On the basis of His holy Word and the divine assurances that He has placed in my heart, I am absolutely convinced that our sovereign God is going to send a great revival to our nation and world and that the Great Commission will be fulfilled. I urge you with every conviction within me—with tears of compassion and commitment, as a matter of life and death for our nation and for the souls of all for whom Christ died—to plan and prepare for revival and help lead a successful fasting and prayer gathering in your church or community.

Preparing Your Leadership

Purpose: To review the need for revival and the importance of fasting and prayer with your leadership team; to provide the main speaker with information to present during the meeting session

Materials: *The Coming Revival*
7 Basic Steps to Successful Fasting and Prayer
Have You Discovered the Wonderful Adventure of the Spirit-Filled Life?
How You Can Pray With Confidence
Handouts 1 and 2

Instructions for this section: Once you have personally studied and applied the material in the *7 Basic Steps to Successful Fasting and Prayer,* you are ready to begin planning your fasting and prayer meeting. The following steps will assist you in conducting your gathering.

1. *Choose several men and women who display godly leadership qualities to help you plan and implement your meetings.* If you are working with a small group, you may want to choose one other person to help you. If you are planning a gathering of more than thirty people, you may need a prayer coordinator, fasting coordinator, main speaker, emcee, and a facilities/finance coordinator. Judge from the size of your prospective groups how big your leadership team should be.

2. *Obtain materials for your leadership team.* This manual and the other materials listed above will help you teach your leadership team and conferees the basics of fasting and prayer and begin a daily habit of seeking God's face. For each person on your team, obtain a copy of this manual and each of the preceding materials. The following two booklets are optional:
How You Can Be Filled With the Holy Spirit
How You Can Walk in the Spirit

Although the information in this manual may be presented without obtaining some of these materials, your team will benefit from having a copy of each. Also available is a video package, *Preparing for the Coming Revival,* which includes messages that will give more training and help for your leaders. The videotapes contain inspiring messages by Nancy Leigh DeMoss and Dr. Henry Blackaby on brokenness, repentance, and reconciliation. These resources are available through your local Christian bookstore, mail-order catalog distributor, or NewLife Publications.

3. *Schedule a training meeting for your group.* Review "What Is Revival?" with them and together discuss the importance of revival personally and as the Body of Christ. As a team:

   ■ Apply the principles in the booklet *Have You Discovered the Wonderful Adventure of the Spirit-Filled Life?* to prepare yourselves spiritually.

   ■ Read through the *7 Basic Steps* booklet together.

   ■ Study this section of your manual and Handouts 1 and 2. Instructions to the leader are in parentheses and italicized.

4. *Hold another meeting to begin planning your gathering.* Assign the following leadership roles, then study the manual sections (shown in parentheses) that apply to each person, either in a one-to-one discussion or as a group:

   Prayer coordinator: Responsible for the prayer seminar, group prayer sessions, and the fasting and prayer chain (The Prayer Seminar and Prayer Coordinator's Guide)

   Fasting coordinator: Responsible for the fasting seminar and the noon fasting prayer group (The Fasting Seminar)

   Main speaker: Responsible for the opening talk (Sections 2 and 4)

   Emcee/Song leader: Responsible for announcements, introductions, Bible reading, and praise and worship (Section 3)

   Facilities/finance coordinator: Responsible for facilities, registration, and refreshments (Section 3)

5. *Plan the details of your gathering.*

   ■ Estimate how many people will attend your gathering.

   ■ Set the date.

   ■ Decide how you will handle the finances.

   ■ Order the amount of material you will need for the conference based on your planned attendance. Each section of this manual lists the materials you will need to conduct that session. Purchase a pocket folder for each person who will attend and place the books, booklets, and handouts inside. I encourage you to provide a copy of *The Coming Revival*, which gives a more complete look at fasting and prayer and the part they play in revival, for each conferee. You may do this by including the book price in the registration fee or by making the book available for sale during the gathering.

- Select a place to hold your gathering and reserve the facilities for the date you set. Make sure the facilities are adequate.
- Plan for break times and the noon break. Since some of the people who attend the gathering may not yet be on a fast, provide ample time for them to get lunch. You will also need to plan a fasting and prayer session during the noon break for those who are fasting. Be sure to provide plenty of water and fruit juices for the breaks, and make them accessible throughout the day.
- Develop publicity.

  Churchwide—flyers, brochures, newsletter announcements

  Target groups—adult Sunday schools, home groups, church boards

  Key people—make personal calls to those whom you wish to attend

The following material explains the basic elements of revival, how to have personal revival, and the importance of fasting. Read this section together or read the section before your meeting and then discuss it when you meet.

What Is Revival?

The Holy Spirit is the author of revival. Ultimately, no Christian is going to fast and pray for a spiritual awakening unless the Spirit leads him to do so (John 6:44). It is the Holy Spirit who convicts of sin (John 16:8).

During revival, the Holy Spirit persuades believers of the holiness, justice, and love of God, and of their need to repent and return to their first love of our Lord. He inspires His servants to speak His messages to the Church. And He uses those whom He inspires to help convince other believers of their need to drop their worldly pursuits and seek after God with all of their hearts.

Therefore, we do not need to wait for a sovereign act of God to bring revival or for a general outpouring of the Holy Spirit. Each believer is already indwelt by the Holy Spirit. Our task is to surrender to the Lordship of Christ and the control of the Holy Spirit, to fast and pray, and to obey God's Word. When we meet these conditions, we can expect the Holy Spirit to transform our lives.

God will send revival to the individual who is willing to repent and seek after Him (Matthew 5:6). God's Word promises us that if we humble ourselves and worship God, He will bless us (Matthew 6:33). Although the Holy Spirit works when and where He chooses, we should always pray, plan, and anticipate His sovereign work in the affairs of people and nations.

Personal revival begins:

- With an inner call to the heart by the Holy Spirit (Philippians 2:13). The conscience finds itself stirred by that call. Our will makes the decision to obey or ignore the leading of the Holy Spirit.
- When we humble ourselves, repent, fast, pray, seek His face, and turn from our evil ways (2 Chronicles 7:14).

Down through the centuries beginning with our Lord's forty-day fast, godly people through whom He has done mighty things have testified to the importance of fasting and prayer in revival. The roll call of great Christian leaders who made prayer with fasting a part of their lives reads like a hall of fame: Martin Luther, John Calvin, John Knox, Jonathan Edwards, John and Charles Wesley, Matthew Henry, Charles Finney, Andrew Murray, D. Martyn Lloyd-Jones, and thousands more. How does fasting cause the fire of God to fall upon the life of the individual and the Church? Let me share six truths about revival, then explain how fasting prepares us for revival.

1. *Revival is a sovereign act of God.* The Holy Spirit orchestrates and enables even our love for Christ. We cannot understand God's Word apart from the Holy Spirit. We cannot pray unless He intercedes for us. We cannot witness for Christ without His power. We cannot live a holy life apart from the Holy Spirit. So, too, revival is the product of the Spirit.

2. *Revival is a divine visitation.* Spiritual renewal was God's idea in the first place. He sent Jesus so that we could experience the fullness of His Spirit within us.

3. *Revival is a time of personal brokenness, humility, forgiveness, and restoration.* It is a time when the Holy Spirit calls a person to repent of obvious sins and reveals those that are not so obvious.

4. *During revival, preaching is fearless* under the anointing of the Holy Spirit. The book of Acts records six times when people were filled with the Holy Spirit. In five of these, the result was boldness in proclaiming the gospel (Acts 4:31).

5. *The presence of the Holy Spirit is powerful.* Fearless, Christ-centered preaching with people "falling on their faces" before God often is a hallmark of revival. In the John Wesley and George Whitfield revivals in England, the awesome presence of the Holy Spirit had a powerful effect on the people.

6. *Revival changes communities and nations.* American theologian A. W. Tozer defines revival as a move of God that "changes the moral climate of a community."[1] History shows that a true awakening leaps far beyond the walls of any church and radically transforms society.

A simple outline of six Rs helps keep these ideas fresh:

- *Recognition* of the greatness of God, His attributes, our unworthiness, and our sin.
- *Repentance* of our sins.
- *Restitution* for the wrongs done to others.
- *Reconciliation* with God and our fellow man.
- *Restoration* to our right relationship with God.
- *Reformation* for us individually and as families, churches, communities, and as a nation.

Our Need to Fast

The writings of Scripture and many Christian leaders offer biblical insights into the spiritual need for fasting:

- It is the only Christian discipline that meets all the conditions of 2 Chronicles 7:14.
- It is a biblical way to humble ourselves in the sight of God (Psalm 35:13; Ezra 8:21).

---

1   Winkie Pratney, *Revival: Its Principles & Personalities* (LaFayette, LA: Huntington House, 1994), p. 17.

- It provides more time to pray, seek God's face, and repent because we are more focused on the Lord and less concerned with daily routines such as preparing meals and eating.
- It brings revelation by the Holy Spirit of our true spiritual condition, leading to brokenness, repentance, and change, and allows the Holy Spirit to work in a most unusual, powerful way.
- It helps us concentrate on the Word of God to make it more meaningful, vital, and practical in our lives.
- It transforms prayer into a richer, more personal experience.
- It can help us regain a strong sense of spiritual determination and restore the loss of our first love for our Lord.

Humility is an attitude of the heart. The Psalmist says, "The Lord is close to those whose hearts are breaking; he rescues those who are humbly sorry for their sins" (Psalm 34:18, TLB). God will hear us and respond to our cry when we come before Him in humility and brokenness—acknowledging and repenting of our sins and asking Him to cleanse us by the blood of Jesus and to fill us with His Holy Spirit.

But you may still wonder, *how does fasting help?*

How Does Fasting Help?

- *Fasting is a primary means of restoration.* Humbling ourselves by fasting releases the Holy Spirit to do His special work of revival in us. This changes our relationship with God forever, taking us into a deeper life in Christ and giving us a greater awareness of God's reality and presence in our lives.
- *Fasting reduces the power of self* so that the Holy Spirit can do a more intense work within us. As a result, He can accomplish His will in us and do "superabundantly" more for us than we could ever imagine.
- *Fasting brings a yieldedness,* even a holy brokenness, resulting in inner calm and self-control. It eliminates some of the physical distractions in our lives, such as preparing and eating food, and can lead to a slower pace and a more peaceful attitude.
- *Fasting renews spiritual vision.* When we feel our life is out of control or have lost our first love for our Lord, fasting can help us focus once again on God's plan for our lives.
- *Fasting inspires determination to follow God's revealed plan for our life.* Perhaps you know what God wants you to do but have a

hard time following through with His plans. Fasting can help strengthen your resolve and keep you on track.

- *Fasting can bring revival to our nation.* The tides of godlessness and lawlessness are rising rapidly in our nation. The sins that led to the Flood of Noah and the destruction of Sodom and Gomorrah have found social acceptance in our society. Clearly, our nation is ripe for judgment. God's judgments of the past are signs for us today. God promises to hear from heaven, forgive our sins, and heal our land (2 Chronicles 7:14) if we as a people are obedient to that call. Nothing less than the supernatural power released when we fast and pray can stem the tides of judgment devastating our land and turn our nation toward God.

But for all its spiritual benefits, fasting is not the easiest godly discipline to practice. For those unaccustomed to it, going without food can be a struggle—a tug of war between the spirit of a person and his flesh.

God's Word declares fasting and prayer to be a powerful means for causing the fire of God to fall again in a person's life. This fire produces the fruits of the Spirit—love, joy, peace, patience, kindness, goodness, faithfulness, gentleness, and self-control—but especially the fruits of righteousness and spiritual power over the lusts of the flesh and the lies of the enemy.

As fasting and prayer brings surrender of body, soul, and spirit to our Lord and Savior Jesus Christ, it also generates a heightened sense of the presence of the Holy Spirit; it creates a fresh, clean joy and a restored determination to serve God. In short, it brings personal revival. And that power is available to all Christians. Just picture your church—and perhaps even your community—becoming unified in purpose, healed of its wounds, and set on fire for God because a group of dedicated members gathered "in one accord" in humility and earnestness before our Lord to fast and pray!

In His Sermon on the Mount, Jesus taught, "When you fast..," not "If you fast." For believers, then, the question is not *Should I fast?*, but *Will I fast?*

I encourage you to prayerfully consider giving a tithe of your day, week, or month to the Lord in fasting and prayer. You will be amazed at how much more you will accomplish in the remaining nine-tenths. Results will show in various ways. God will help you increase your efficiency. Others may offer to help you with a time-consuming project. The demands on your time may lessen. Certainly you will discover that your other Christian duties will increase in fruitfulness, and you will be more effective in sharing your faith with your loved ones, friends, and neighbors.

(Encourage your team members to use Handouts 1 and 2 as they prepare for the gathering and in the days following the event.)

The Fasting Seminar

Purpose: To prepare conferees with an understanding of how to fast and to motivate them to begin fasting to bring revival

Materials: *7 Basic Steps to Successful Fasting and Prayer*
Have You Made the Wonderful Discovery of the Spirit-Filled Life?

Instructions for this section: As conferees arrive for the seminar, make sure each person has a copy of both booklets. Explain that their contribution to discussion is important to you so they should feel free to speak up. Then begin your session in prayer. Present the material, allowing conferees to respond and interact during the session. The leader's directions for leading the seminar are in parentheses and italicized throughout the lesson. At the close of your seminar, offer a prayer of consecration for everyone who plans on beginning a fast. You may want to write down each name so you can pray for them over the next few weeks.

Use the following material as a basis for guiding discussion and giving information on fasting. You may want to use a chalkboard or flip chart to write the points as they are given.

Preparing Your Heart to Fast and Pray

Perhaps many of you are wondering, "What is fasting? How will it help me in my walk with God?" What does fasting mean to you? *(Pause for discussion.)*

Fasting prepares us for the deepest and richest spiritual communion possible. It clears and liberates our minds to understand what God is saying to our spirits. It conditions our bodies to carry out His perfect will.

When we persevere through the initial mental and physical discomforts, we experience a calming of the soul and cooling of the appetites. As a result, we sense the presence of the Lord in a very special way. We begin to see the fruit of His Holy Spirit evidenced in a fresh, new way (Galatians 5:22,23).

Many who write about the values of fasting point to increased effectiveness in intercessory prayer, deliverance from spiritual bondage, and guidance in decisions. Since spiritual fasting helps bring the soul more in tune with God, it enables us to meet His conditions for answered prayer (1 John 3:21,22).

Spiritual fasting consists of the following:

- *Focusing on God.* Our prayers bring results only when our hearts are pure and our motives are unselfish. This can take place only if God and His holy Word are at the center of our attention (James 4:8,10). A humble heart is repentant, dependent upon the Holy Spirit, grateful, forgiving, obedient, respectful, and willing to serve. Prayer with fasting intensifies these and other inner workings of the Holy Spirit.

- *Waiting for the leading of the Lord.* If you undertake a long fast simply on your own in the energy of your flesh, you may run into difficulties. But if the Lord leads you into a protracted fast, He will give you the strength to carry it out. You are free to "proclaim" a fast whenever you sense the desire to draw close to God in a dynamic way or feel the need to seek special help from Him.

- *Presenting our bodies "as living sacrifices, holy and pleasing to God"* (Romans 12:1). We crucify our sinful desires so that we can more effectively serve God and fulfill His will in our lives.

- *Praying for ourselves and interceding for others.* We bring our personal needs before the Lord and intercede for our loved ones, friends, church, community, nation, and the world— and that the Great Commission will be fulfilled.

Once you understand the purpose of fasting and realize what it does for you, regular fasting will begin to make spiritual sense. The more you fast to seek God's face and His glory, the more you will want to fast. The rewards and benefits are rich beyond measure. Let us look at several steps you can take during a spiritual fast.

7 Steps to Successful Fasting and Prayer

How you begin your fast will determine your success. The following seven steps will make your time with the Lord more meaningful and spiritually rewarding, while at the same time enhancing your physical health:

1. Set your objectives.
2. Ask the Holy Spirit to reveal the kind of fast God wants you to undertake.
3. Prepare yourself spiritually.

4. Prepare yourself physically.
5. Put yourself on a schedule.
6. End your fast gradually.
7. Expect results.

Let's read through the *7 Basic Steps* booklet to learn how to apply these steps. Feel free to discuss those areas that are new to you.

(If your students do not already have booklets, distribute them now. Also hand out the booklet Have You Made the Wonderful Discovery of the Spirit-Filled Life? *Read through the 7 Basic Steps with your conferees. If you have time, discuss the appendix "How to Experience and Maintain Personal Revival" and discuss the six vital questions about prayer.*

When you finish, explain that the booklet Have You Made the Wonderful Discovery of the Spirit-Filled Life? *teaches how to walk in the Spirit as a way of life. Read through this booklet also, highlighting "Spiritual Breathing" on page 15.*

Conclude the seminar with the following statement.)

Most people experience a measure of revival as a result of fasting. But just as we need fresh infillings of the Holy Spirit daily, we also need new times of fasting before God. A single fast is not a spiritual cure-all. John and Charles Wesley advocated fasting two days a week to "keep the flesh under" and to maintain the closeness with God that fasting brings. I encourage you to fast with prayer again and again and again until we truly experience revival in our homes, our churches, our beloved nation, and in the world.

(God has impressed me to pray for two million North Americans who will fast for forty days for revival and the fulfillment of the Great Commission. Ask the Holy Spirit if you are to be one of the two million. Then encourage the members of your team to make this same commitment. Close in prayer that your hearts will be revived to do God's work.)

Prayer Coordinator's Guide

Purpose: To help the prayer coordinator conduct the prayer sessions during the gathering

Materials: Handouts 3 and 4

Instructions for this section: During the group prayer session of the gathering, distribute Handout 3. Use Handout 4 during the Fasting and Prayer Chain announcement.

Guidelines for Teaching Group Prayer

1. Introduce praying aloud by explaining the following:

   It is hard for many people to pray aloud. Children will be frank enough to say, "I don't like to pray aloud," or "I don't know what to say." On the other hand, many adults feel the need to pray but hesitate to come to a meeting where there will be prayer because they feel like the children, but are afraid to admit it. Only God has the answers to all of our troubles, and He has instructed us to come to Him as little children. When you pray aloud in your group, do not be afraid to admit your fear. Instead, make your first prayer one for strength and courage.

2. Instruct individuals by saying:

   - Be honest in prayer. Say "I" when you mean "I"; say "we" when you mean "we."
   - Do not try to impress others when you pray.
   - Talk things over with God as with a friend.
   - Include expressions of love and adoration such as "I love You, Lord."
   - During one of the break times, find a solitary place and pray aloud so that you can become accustomed to hearing the sound of your voice in prayer.
   - Write out your prayers and bring them to read aloud in your prayer group. This will help you remember what you want to say when praying aloud.

Conducting a Spontaneous Prayer Session

1. Divide the participants into groups of four to six people.
2. Ask group members to introduce themselves.
3. Allow a brief time to get acquainted.
4. Guide the prayer time by instructing everyone to:
   - Verbalize a short, simple prayer in ten words or less.
   - Talk to God as you would to a friend present in the group. Conversational prayer is the expression of the human heart in conversation with God.
   - Speak in modern conversational language. The more natural your prayer, the more real God becomes to you.
   - Avoid making a "prayer speech" or "preaching" at others during prayer.
   - Pray as often as you wish, but avoid monopolizing the time. It is not necessary to pray around the circle.
   - Experienced pray-ers, keep your prayers short and simple. You may struggle to be simple as much as the beginner struggles to verbalize. This will enhance rapport and help prevent the timid individual from feeling intimidated.
5. Direct participants in conversational prayer by introducing the following prayer conversations one at a time:
   - "Thank you" for one thing, such as the Lord Jesus, God's love, His forgiveness, your family, pastor, friends, and so forth.
   - "Thank you" for something that has happened in your life in the last 24 hours.
   - "Please help..." (yourself or someone else).
   - Ask for one thing for yourself.
   - Thank God for how He will meet those desires and requests.
6. Continue praying spontaneously, introducing requests during prayer and allowing an opportunity for others to pray on a single subject until everyone who wants to participate has done so.
   - As the Holy Spirit directs, allow everyone to pray who wants to pray.
   - Don't be concerned about silence—God speaks in silence.
   - Let God speak to you.
7. Close with a final prayer of thanksgiving, acknowledging God's faithfulness, love, and sovereignty.

Introducing Variety Into Prayer Sessions

1. Utilize various resources to give instruction on prayer.

    ■ Use a different prayer topic for each group prayer session. Handouts 3 and 6 can help groups pray for different kinds of people and needs.

    ■ Utilize resources such as a Bible dictionary, concordance, and commentaries to expand your understanding of prayer, then present prayer principles at the beginning of a session. Limit your presentation to 10–15 minutes.

    ■ Ask participants to look up specific passages on prayer.

    ■ Refer to and claim specific verses of Scripture for particular requests.

2. Pray through the Scriptures:

    ■ Choose a passage of Scripture or a psalm of praise such as Psalm 103 or a passage from Psalms 145–150.

    ■ Teach the group to pray using the following procedure:

    The first person reads a phrase or entire verse aloud, pausing to verbalize a simple prayer as inspired by the Scripture and led by the Lord.

    Other members of the group join in audibly or silently agree.

    Another person continues reading the next verse, pausing to pray aloud as he or she is impressed by the Lord.

    Continue in a similar fashion around the group.

3. Introduce the ACTS acrostic. (This can be developed at length with one or more studies on each word.) Guide the prayer time praying silently or aloud, except always pray silently for personal confession.

    ■ *Adoration:* Worshiping and praising God, exalting Him with your lips and in your heart and mind. Read Psalms such as 103. Take time to adore God, praising Him for His attributes such as His lovingkindness, His holiness, His compassion, His majesty, etc.

    ■ *Confession:* Agreeing with God concerning any sins He brings to mind in order to restore fellowship with Him. Review 1 John 1:5–9. As you spend time adoring God, He will bring to mind what you need to confess.

    ■ *Thanksgiving:* Rendering thanksgiving to God, a prayer expressing gratitude. Read 1 Thessalonians 5:18; Ephesians 5:20;

Psalm 50:23. Spend time thanking God for His attributes, His gifts to us, and many other things.

- *Supplication:* Presenting needs to God, for yourself and others. Read Philippians 4:6,7; Psalm 116:1,2. Lead the group in supplication, praying aloud.

4. Introduce the PRAY acrostic (may be developed in the same way as ACTS).
   - Praise
   - Repent
   - Ask for someone else
   - Your own needs

Praying in One Accord

1. Emphasize that when the early church prayed in one accord, they turned the world upside down (Acts 4:24,31; 17:5–7).
2. Describe how an earthquake opened prison doors for Paul and Silas when they prayed together (Acts 16:25,26).
3. Remind conferees that Jesus Christ Himself is actually present with them. Read His promises in Matthew 18:19,20.
4. Give individuals the following instructions:
   - Concentrate on what the other person is praying, agreeing in your heart. Do not be thinking ahead to what you will pray. You will miss the other person's prayer and neglect to pray in one accord.
   - Trust the Holy Spirit to direct your thoughts and prayer when it is your turn.

Encouraging Individuals to Pray Continuously

1. Remind conferees that God commands us to pray without ceasing (1 Thessalonians 5:17).
2. Encourage them to recognize that God is present wherever they go and that He is always ready to answer prayer. Practice the presence of God as a way of life.
3. Talk about how important it is to thank God for everything He allows into our lives (1 Thessalonians 5:18)—from a beautiful day to a flat tire. (Your prayers can be a good example. Keep them simple, sincere, brief, and reflecting your faith.)

4. Encourage conferees to talk to God when they feel a need—any time of the day or night.

5. Suggest they use their time more wisely by developing a habit of praying during daily activities that do not require total concentration, such as showering, driving, or gardening.

The Prayer Seminar

Purpose: To teach conferees the importance of prayer and how to pray effectively

Materials: Handouts 4 and 5

Instructions for this section: During this seminar, present the following material and discuss the handouts. Additional material may be presented by using Handout 6.

Results of Learning How to Pray Scripturally

1. God will answer your prayers (Matthew 7:7).
2. You will achieve personal holiness and moral strength. Prayerlessness results in a powerless spiritual life.
3. You will be cleansed in spirit.
4. You will learn how to worship and express adoration for God as the psalmists did.
5. You will pray more effectively.
6. Your relationship with God will become deeper through answered prayer.
7. You will pray with greater faith and confidence in God's promise to hear and answer your prayer.
8. You will become more fruitful in your witness for Christ.

Establishing a Daily, Personal Communion With God

1. Recognize why you need a quiet time alone with God. You will be following Christ's example (Mark 1:35).
   - Frequent and regular time alone with someone is needed to develop any relationship.
   - Unlimited spiritual resources are available to the person who spends time alone with God.
   - The Christian is engaged in a spiritual battle and needs the strengthening and refreshing that comes from spending time with God. Spiritual food cannot be "stored up."
   - Time alone with the Lord, preferably as you begin your day, sets a spiritual tone for the day.

2. Set aside a regular time to be alone with God. Select a time when you are alert. Early morning has many advantages. To J. Hudson Taylor, "Prayer in the morning is like tuning the orchestra before the symphony begins." Note the example of David: "In the morning I lay my requests before you and wait in expectation" (Psalm 5:3).

3. Choose a quiet spot and make it the place you meet with God daily. Avoid noise and distraction.

4. Have a pencil and paper handy to jot down intruding thoughts of "things to do."

5. Allow unhindered time for God to speak to your heart.
    - Let Him speak through His Word and, occasionally, from hymns and devotional material. Use a variety of methods.
    - Wait quietly before Him.
    - Spend time in prayer speaking to Him.

6. Focus on the quality of your relationship to God rather than the amount of time you spend in prayer. Meeting God is your objective, not preparing for a Sunday school class or other activity.

7. Do not be mechanical or legalistic. If you miss your quiet time, confess it, thank God for His forgiveness, and continue to walk in the Spirit. Do not be bound by guilt. A daily quiet time is not a good luck charm to make the day go right. Our greatest desire should be to spend as much time with God as possible because we love Him and want to be with Him.

8. Invite God to build a daily quiet time as a regular discipline into your life. Ask Him to make you continually hunger and thirst for Him (Matthew 5:6).

9. Ask God to give you His wisdom for working out the details of your daily quiet time. He knows what is best for you.

10. Be rested when you meet with God. Go to bed on time. Before you fall asleep, read a passage or two of what you intend to study the next day and meditate on it as you go to sleep.

11. Periodically, set aside an entire day for the sole purpose of seeking after the Lord in prayer.

Conducting Your Fasting and Prayer Gathering

Purpose: To plan and conduct a fasting and prayer gathering

Materials: Handouts 6–9

Any of the other handouts that you would like to use during group prayer sessions

Instructions for this section: Now that you have prepared yourself through fasting and prayer and have chosen and trained leaders to help you, you are ready to hold your fasting and prayer gathering. This section contains two parts. The first, "When Revival Comes," is material for personal motivation. You may also present this material during one of the praise and worship times.

The second part, "Schedule for a Friday–Saturday Gathering," gives an example of how you can plan a gathering for a Friday night through Saturday. Adjust the schedule to fit your needs, keeping in mind that the majority of your time should be spent in personal and group prayer. Keep the praise and worship times prayerful also.

The schedule lists times when the seminars may be appropriate. Use the handouts listed above during the group prayer times. Use the seminar handouts received in the fasting and prayer seminars during the group and personal prayer sessions later in the gathering. Instructions to the leader are in parentheses and italicized.

May God bless you as you conduct your gathering.

When Revival Comes

If awakenings of the past foreshadow events to come, I believe we will see the fire of the Holy Spirit break out in our churches and spread to every nook and cranny in the land. We will see revival begin with God's people, but millions of unbelievers everywhere—in government, education, the media, Hollywood—will turn to Christ in unprecedented numbers. That is the nature of true revival. It is never contained within church walls.

As this revival sweeps throughout our nation and around the world, we will see renewed religious fervor. There will be greater reverence for God and a fresh awareness of the awesomeness of God and His attributes, a restoration of true worship, a hunger for the Word of God, and a new zeal to tell others about our Lord Jesus Christ and the Good News of God's love and forgiveness. In fact, if what is perceived as "revival" does not result in massive evangelization, it is not a true revival. We also will see a renewed vision for social issues and racial reconciliation.

When revival comes, Christians will exercise greater influence in their communities and in our nation. As a result of fasting and prayer and personal revival, they will:

- Demonstrate the supernatural love of God in their personal lives, their homes, their churches, and in all of their secular relationships.

- Become actively involved in restoring every facet of society, including government, to the biblical values of our Founding Fathers.

- Cease supporting the immorality-makers by avoiding movies, home videos, and television programs that patronize lust, illicit sex, and violence.

- Influence the media by encouraging secular broadcasters and editors to present a fair and balanced view of the religious community.

- Support Christian organizations committed to restoring our vital freedoms.

- Help their politicians know what they stand for and seek to elect those who live upright lives and fight for moral causes.

- Work harder to restore godly standards for right and wrong in our educational system.

What can you do to help prepare for revival?

Schedule for a Friday–Saturday Gathering

Allot the following amount of time to each activity:

    15–20 percent in music, worship, and short Bible reading
    10–15 percent in instructions and announcements
    20 percent in speaking sessions and seminars
    10 percent in personal prayer
    40 percent in group prayer and prayer requests

Friday night

 Registration (start one hour before opening session)
 Opening session (1 hour):
  Announcements, introductions, opening prayer (15 minutes)
  (The Prayer for Revival on page 34 can be used to open the session.)
  Praise and worship, including Bible reading (15 minutes)
  Main speaker's talk (20–30 minutes) *(The message should emphasize some facet of fasting, prayer, or revival. Portions of the video package* Preparing for the Coming Revival *can be used in place of the main speaker's address, during a session, or as reference material for the speaker.)*
 Break (15 minutes)
 Prayer groups (1 hour 15 minutes):
  Prayer for revival; use Handout 9 (25 minutes)
  Prayer for community; use Handout 6 (15 minutes)
  Prayer for church; use Handout 7 (15 minutes)
  Prayer for nation; use Handout 8 (20 minutes)
 Closing session (30 minutes):
  Praise and worship, including Bible reading (15 minutes)
  Announcements, closing prayer (15 minutes)

Saturday session

 Opening session (45 minutes):
  Announcements, opening prayer (10 minutes)
  Praise and worship, including Bible reading (25 minutes)
  Introduction to fasting and prayer seminars (10 minutes)
 Fasting seminar (30 minutes)
 Break (15 minutes)
 Personal prayer; use Handout 9 (30 minutes)
 Prayer groups (1 hour)
 Noon break (1 hour) *(Or prayer time for those already on a fast.)*
 Opening session (15 minutes):
  Praise and worship (10 minutes)
  Introduction to prayer seminar (5 minutes)
 Prayer seminar (30 minutes)
 Personal prayer (30 minutes)
 Prayer groups (1 hour)
 Praise and worship (15 minutes)
 Introduction of fasting and prayer chain (15 minutes) *(Provide sign-up sheets for attendees to join small fasting and prayer groups.)*

Prayer groups (45 minutes) *(Ask those who signed up for fasting and prayer groups to meet with their new group.)*

Concluding session (45 minutes):

Praise and worship, including Bible reading (20 minutes)

Announcements (5 minutes)

Closing prayer (5 minutes)

Closing challenge (15 minutes) *(Have the main speaker challenge conferees to seek God's face more consistently through fasting and prayer.)*

A Prayer for Revival

Our Father God, we come before Your throne to humble ourselves and pray, to seek Your face and turn from our wicked ways.

We have sinned against You, O Lord. As individuals and as a nation, we have disobeyed Your clear commands. We have not loved You with all of our heart, soul, mind, and strength. We have not loved our neighbors as we love ourselves; we have not loved our enemies.

Forgive us, O God. Send a spirit of repentance. Heal our land. Let it sweep across this nation. Let the purging fire of revival begin in my heart and in Your Church. Let it spread through every community, every town, and every city in our land and around the world.

Establish righteousness, we pray. Let the bad roots that produce the bad fruits be burned out of our lives. Father, we ask that godly leaders will be raised up and elected to public office at every level. And that ungodly leaders will be removed. May Satan's hold on government be broken and righteous rule be established. We pray that your Word will be invited back into our houses, our schools, and in every facet of our society. May Your kingdom come and Your will be done on earth as it is in heaven.

This prayer we earnestly pray in the name of Jesus and for the glory of God. Amen.

(Adapted from a prayer given by Thomas Trask, general superintendent of the General Council of the Assemblies of God, during a fasting and prayer gathering in Orlando, Florida.)

SECTION 4

Resources

Aldrich, Joe. (1992). *Prayer Summits*. Portland: Multnomah.

Barnhouse, D. G. (1965). *The Invisible War*. Grand Rapids, MI: Zondervan.

Bragg, Paul & Patricia. (nd). *The Miracle of Fasting*. Santa Barbara: Health Science.

Bright, Bill. (1994). *The Christian and Prayer*. Orlando, FL: NewLife Publications.

Bright, Bill. (1991). *How You Can Walk in the Spirit*. Orlando, FL: NewLife Publications.

Bright, V. & Jennings, B. (1989). *Unleashing the Power of Prayer*. Chicago: Moody.

Campus Crusade for Christ. (1975). *Prayer Handbook*. Orlando, FL: Campus Crusade for Christ.

Chatham, R. D. (1987). *Fasting: A Biblical-Historical Study*. South Plainfield, NJ: Bridge.

Carson, D. A. (1990). *Teach Us to Pray*. Grand Rapids, MI: Baker.

Duewel, W. L. (1986). *Touch the World Through Prayer*. Grand Rapids, MI: Zondervan.

Finney, C. G. (1984, reprint from 1833). *How to Experience Revival*. Springdale, PA: Whittaker House.

Getz, Gene. (1982). *Praying for One Another*. Wheaton, IL: Victor Books.

Great Commission Prayer Crusade. (1978). *Personal Prayer Diary*. Orlando, FL: Campus Crusade for Christ.

Hayes, Dan. (1983). *Fireseeds of Spiritual Awakening*. Orlando, FL: Campus Crusade for Christ.

Jennings, Ben. (1992). *International Prayer Curriculum*. Orlando, FL: International Prayer Ministry, Campus Crusade for Christ.

Killingsworth, Laurie. (1995). *Passionate Hearts: A Prayer Conference for Women*. Orlando, FL: New Life Center, Campus Crusade for Christ.

Lloyd-Jones, Martin. (1987). *Revival*. Wheaton, IL: Crossway.

McKenna, David L. (1990). *The Coming Great Awakening*. Downers Grove, IL: IVP.

Murray, Andrew. (1981, reprint). *With Christ in the School of Prayer*. Springdale, PA: Whittaker House.

Orr, J. Edwin. (1974). *The Fervent Prayer*. Chicago: Moody.

Sanders, J. O. (1977). *Prayer Power Unlimited*. Chicago: Moody.

Schaffer, Edith. (1992). *The Life of Prayer*. Wheaton, IL: Crossway.

Stanley, Charles. (1985). *How to Listen to God*. Nashville: Thomas Nelson.

Stedman, Ray. (1975). *Jesus Teaches on Prayer*. Waco, TX: Word.

Wallis, Arthur. (1993). *God's Chosen Fast*. Fort Washington, PA: Christian Literature Crusade.

Wesley, John. (1987, reprint). *The Nature of Revival*. Compiled by Clare George Weakley, Jr. Minneapolis: Bethany.

Handout 1

How to Establish a Fasting and Prayer Movement Within Your Church

1. Give prayer priority in the church: "My house will be called a house of prayer for all nations" (Isaiah 56:7).

2. The pastor and church staff must have a vision for the involvement of their members in a vital prayer ministry. They need to see their role from Ephesians 4:11–13 as that of "preparing God's people for works of service." The pastor should also set the example by his personal prayer life, leadership, and involvement.

3. Establish a prayer ministry in your church, giving it the same level of influence as other ministries such as youth, adults, women, etc.

4. Challenge a potential prayer leadership group to commit themselves to give training and personal involvement in prayer a priority. The criteria for selecting this leadership group should include trained members who have:

   - A vision for affecting and reaching their community through prayer
   - Effective personal prayer lives
   - Leadership potential
   - A schedule not already heavily burdened with responsibility

Handout 2

How to Experience and Maintain Revival in Your Church

Join us in prayer and fasting that God will bring about a greater knowledge of Christ than we have ever seen before, that millions of Christians will live holy lives, and that our nation will be turned back to biblical foundations and spiritual lifestyles.

1. Encourage your pastor and church leaders to preach and teach on the attributes of God as a basis for first love, faith, and obedience.

2. Organize a 24-hour prayer chain divided into 96 fifteen-minute periods. Ask participants to pray for revival among church members and for a great spiritual harvest of new believers.

3. Choose seven church members to meet with the pastor early each Sunday morning for prayer and to receive his prayer requests for each day of the week.

4. Invite several church members to gather for prayer during each church service, especially while the pastor is preaching.

5. Encourage all church members to fast and pray on behalf of the pastor and the church for one 24-hour period each week.

6. Ask your pastor or church leader to emphasize biblical truths on repentance, confession of sin, restitution, and reconciliation among church members.

7. Teach members how to be filled with the Holy Spirit and walk in the fullness and power of the Holy Spirit by faith as a way of life.

8. Train church members and other Christian groups on an ongoing basis to share their faith more effectively in the power of the Holy Spirit.

9. Designate one night each week for positive, aggressive evangelism as a part of church visitation.

10. Challenge members to help fulfill the Great Commission in their neighborhood and develop a vision for the world. Since God's great heart is committed to world evangelism, He will especially bless the church that has a major emphasis on helping to fulfill the Great Commission. Designate a significant percentage of the church budget to evangelism outside the United States. (Many

churches designate 25 to 50 percent of their total church budget to overseas missions.)

11. Encourage members to honor the Lord through obedient and faithful stewardship. Teach them the joy of giving tithes and offerings.

12. Teach the history and conditions of revival. Encourage members to read biblical and historical accounts of revival.

Handout 3
Scripture References for Specific Prayer

Yourself: Pray for pure thoughts and deeds, that you may be a channel for God's love where you live, work, and worship. *Colossians 1:9-12; Philippians 4:8; 2 Corinthians 2:14,15; 1 Peter 1:13–16.*

Your Home and Family: Pray for a Christ-centered home and family. Seek God's wisdom and guidance in applying His principles. *Ephesians 4:31,32; 5:22–6:4; 1 Peter 3:8,9; Proverbs 3:33; Psalm 127:1.*

The Church: Pray for unity within the church and Christian organizations. Pray that Christians will witness for Christ through their lives and words. *Philippians 2:1–7; John 17:11; Ephesians 4:1–3,11–16; 1 Corinthians 12:12,13; 2 Corinthians 2:14–17; 5:14–21.*

The Community: Pray for a Christian ministry of reconciliation in your community. *1 Corinthians 10:24; 2 Corinthians 2:14–16; 3:5; 5:17–20; Jeremiah 33:3–8; Psalm 127:1.*

The Nation: Pray for national repentance, acknowledging God's mercy and forgiveness. *2 Chronicles 7:14; 13:12; 15:2; 20:3–6,12; 24:20; 30:12; Ezekiel 8:17,18; Ezra 8:21–23.*

The World: Pray for a spirit of revival to sweep the world, that the nations will worship the Lord with reverence. *Psalm 2; 33:8,10–12.*

Those in Authority: Pray that the leaders of our country have wisdom, integrity, protection, guidance. *1 Timothy 1:6; 2:1–6; 1 Corinthians 2:5; 3:18–20; Romans 13:1; 1 Samuel 12:14,15; Jeremiah 33:3.*

Non-Believers: Pray that the lost will be freed from the enemy, enlightened through the gospel, granted repentance, and drawn to the Father. *Romans 6:19–23; 10:1,13–15; 1 Timothy 2:4–6; 2 Timothy 2:25,26; Revelation 3:20; John 8:36; 2 Corinthians 3:17.*

The Sick, Discouraged, and Persecuted: Pray for God's mercy, strength, and lovingkindness. Pray that they may be aware of His presence. *Acts 3:16; Philippians 2:27; James 5:14,15; 1 Peter 5:7; 2 Corinthians 1:3,4; 4:16,17; 12:8–10; Psalm 118:5,6; Ephesians 5:20.*

The Media: Pray for Christian influence in newspapers, magazines, television, and movies. *Colossians 2:8; Proverbs 1:7; 15:26,28,31.*

Students and Teachers: Pray for teachers to teach biblical principles and values, and for students to honor the Lord through pure lives. *Ephesians 3:13–19; 5:1–4; Psalm 1:1–3; 16:11; 37:23,24.*

Handout 4
How to Build a Fasting and Prayer Chain

A fasting and prayer chain is a group of people who agree to uphold one another by spending time each week in fasting and prayer. Unlike a telephone prayer chain, a church fasting and prayer chain will continuously uphold the leaders and people of the church and will meet to praise and worship God. Use the following steps to build a fasting and prayer chain in your church:

1. *Seek the involvement of the pastors and leaders of the church.*

2. If you are holding a gathering in your church, *set out a table with a sign-up sheet for the fasting and prayer chain.* Pass the sheet around during the time when you introduce the chain for your church.

3. *Gather groups of no more than ten people per group and meet once a week* to fast and pray for revival in your church and community. Keep the time to one hour, unless everyone in the group wants to spend longer.

4. As you share personal needs for prayer, *assign someone to record them and mail a list of prayer needs to group members,* so they can continue in prayer throughout the week. If someone mentions a request but does not want it written down, honor his request.

5. *In your weekly prayer time, include the following:*
   - Bible reading and praise
   - Thanksgiving for the previous week's prayer requests
   - Confession and openness to God
   - New petitions
   - Encouraging each other in fasting

6. *As the group grows in numbers, split the group.* Schedule the new group meeting at another time or place to allow others to attend who cannot fit the first meeting into their schedules.

Each group will take on its own identity. Your group may wish to designate a day of the week as a time for fasting. This will bring the whole group together in pursuit of God through fasting and prayer.

Handout 5
How to Pray Without Hindrance

1. Resist the enemy (Ephesians 6:11; James 4:7).
   - Hide God's Word in your heart (Psalm 119:11).
   - Humble yourself before God (1 Peter 5:6–9, James 4:10).
2. Maintain harmony in your relationships (1 Peter 3:7–12).
3. Abide in Christ and His Word (John 15:7).
4. Praise God. God inhabits the praise of His people (Psalm 22:3). Praise is your greatest defense against Satan.
5. Claim Christ's authority over evil (Galatians 1:3,4).

How to Pray With a Partner

1. Ask God to lead you to someone who will be your prayer partner (someone of the same sex or possibly your spouse).
2. Meet regularly for prayer:
   - Each week in person (for example, businessmen could meet for breakfast or lunch or during break time).
   - Three or more times each week over the phone (plan a certain time to call each other for a brief time of sharing and praying aloud).

Handout 6
How to Pray for Your Community

Prayer for our communities is biblical. Moses, Joshua, David, and many of the prophets prayed for their communities and nations and encouraged others to pray (Exodus 32:31,32; Joshua 7:6–9; Psalm 147). Paul encourages us to pray against strongholds of spiritual wickedness and to pray for our leaders, families, and the evangelization of those who need Jesus (Philippians 1:1–11).

Adopt a target audience for whom to fast and pray, ranging in size from one thousand people to no more than one million people. Even in large cities of two or three million, the most manageable size is one million. We call this a Million Person Target Area. This will be your prayer and evangelism community.

You can help the small fasting and prayer groups in your church by collecting and making available the following information from your target area:

- Names of all local government officials
- Names of all school board members and school principals
- Names of all church leaders and pastors
- All groups that support godliness and righteousness
- All groups or establishments that promote unrighteousness, whether legal or illegal
- All groups that promote spiritualism or demonic activity, or buildings where such activity has occurred

Ask fasting and prayer groups to pray systematically for each area of community concern that your central fasting and prayer group identifies. As particular needs are presented, these groups will want to fast and pray for the need and for revival in Christ's Body.

Handout 7
How to Accelerate Prayer in Your Church

1. Guidelines for accelerating prayer in your church
   - Recognize the local church as God's primary instrument for evangelizing our communities and discipling believers. The purpose of the church is:

     To glorify Christ
     To make mature witnessing disciples of all of its members
     To reach every non-Christian in the community with the Good News of Jesus Christ

   - Make prayer a vital part of evangelism and discipleship in your church. Prayer is the key to seeing God work in:

     The lives of individuals and churches
     Our city, nation, and world

   - Ask God to begin a prayer movement in your church. This is necessary if the church is going to see its purpose of evangelism and discipleship fulfilled. Dr. Vernon Grounds of the Conservative Baptist Seminary in Denver says, "The average layman is praying less than five minutes per day."

   - Envision in your mind's eye what can happen in a local church where a prayer movement is taking place. Ask yourself:

     What happened in the early church?
     What is happening in other churches?
     What can happen in my church?

   - Initiate a movement of prayer in your church, not just a successfully developed program of prayer.

2. Results of accelerating prayer in the church
   - Something new and special takes place in a body of believers who learn to pray in one accord.
   - A strong prayer base increases unity and excitement among all who participate.
   - As God answers united prayer, both faith and ministries grow.

Handout 8

How to Encourage and Sustain Revival in Our Nation

1. Organize prayer groups in homes and churches to fast and pray for revival and to study biblical and historical examples of revival.

2. Encourage publishers, owners, and managers of the Christian print media across our land to emphasize fasting and prayer for revival.

3. Encourage all pastors and religious leaders, especially those with access to the electronic and print media, to devote 50 percent of their messages and articles to some facet of revival.

4. Pray specifically for the conversion and revival of all who have influence over others in politics, from the precinct to the White House; in education, at all levels of faculty and students; in religion; in all branches of the military; in athletics; in the broadcast and print media; in the entertainment industry—television, film, music, and the arts; in advertising, business, finance, industry, labor, medicine, law, and in other professional areas.

5. Emphasize our biblical, Judeo-Christian roots and national heritage in churches, schools, and civic organizations.

6. Encourage Christian broadcasters to present quality prime-time programs on fasting, prayer, and revival on secular and Christian radio and television stations.

7. Encourage more aggressive efforts to present the "most joyful news" to every nonbeliever in our nation while at the same time presenting the message of revival to believers.

8. Enlist nationally-known Christian leaders in entertainment, athletics, business, and politics to take leadership in communicating the message of fasting and prayer for revival across our nation.

Handout 9
Proud Spirits and Humble Hearts

Nancy Leigh DeMoss contrasts characteristics of proud, unbroken people who are resistant to the call of God on their lives with the qualities of broken, humble people who have experienced God's revival. Read each item on the list as you ask God to reveal which characteristics of a proud spirit He finds in your life. Confess these to Him, then ask Him to restore the corresponding quality of a broken, humble spirit in you.

Proud, Unbroken People	Broken People
Focus on the failure of others	Overwhelmed with a sense of their own spiritual need
Self-righteous; have a critical, fault-finding spirit; look at own life/faults through a telescope but at others with a microscope	Compassionate; forgiving; look for best in others
Look down on others	Esteem all others better than self
Independent/self-sufficient spirit	Dependent spirit/recognize need for others
Maintain control; must be my way	Surrender control
Have to prove that they are right	Willing to yield the right to be right
Claim rights	Yield rights
Demanding spirit	Giving spirit
Desire to be served	Motivated to serve others
Desire for self-advancement	Desire to promote others
Driven to be recognized/appreciated	Sense of unworthiness; thrilled to be used at all; eager for others to get credit
Wounded when others are promoted and they are overlooked	Rejoice when others are lifted up
"The ministry is privileged to have me!"	"I don't deserve to serve in this ministry!"
Think of what they can do for God	Know that they have nothing to offer God
Feel confident in how much they know	Humbled by how much they have to learn

Proud, Unbroken People	Broken People
Self-conscious	Not concerned with self at all
Keep people at arm's length	Risk getting close to others; willing to take the risk of loving intimately
Quick to blame others	Accept personal responsibility— can see where they are wrong
Unapproachable	"Easy to be entreated"
Defensive when criticized	Receive criticism with a humble, open heart
Concerned with being "respectable"	Concerned with being real
Concerned about what others think	All that matters is what God knows
Work to maintain image/protect reputation	Die to own reputation
Find it difficult to share their spiritual needs with others	Willing to be open/transparent with others
Want to be sure nobody finds out about their sin	Willing to be exposed (Once broken, you don't care who knows—nothing to lose)
Have a hard time saying, "I was wrong; will you please forgive me?"	Quick to admit failure and to seek forgiveness
When confessing sin, deal in generalities	Deal in specifics
Concerned about the consequences of their sins	Grieved over the cause/root of their sins
Remorseful over their sin—got caught/found out	Repentant over sin (forsake it)
When there is a misunderstanding or conflict, wait for the other to come and ask forgiveness	Take the initiative to be reconciled; see if they can get to the cross first!
Compare themselves with others and feel deserving of honor	Compare themselves to the holiness of God and feel desperate need for mercy
Don't think they have anything to repent of	Continual heart attitude of repentance
Don't think they need revival (think everybody else does)	Continually sense their need for a fresh encounter with the filling of the Holy Spirit

Our nation is in a moral free-fall and the Church for the most part is spiritually impotent. What can we do to stop the tragic decline? This book gives the startling answer! Easy-to-read. The thoughts are fresh. The challenge is compelling. (224 pp., $9.99)

This handy reference guide to fasting and prayer is available alone or as a companion to *The Coming Revival*. (24 pp., $4.95/pkg. 5)

How You Can Pray With Confidence. Based on life-changing biblical truths, this booklet provides practical and powerful steps to deeper communion with God. Part of the Transferable Concept series. (64 pp., $1.99)

How You Can Be Filled With the Holy Spirit. This time-tested booklet provides insight on the dynamic process of being filled with the Holy Spirit. This booklet shows how to live with a new dimension of happiness and joy every day. Part of the Transferable Concept series. (64 pp., $1.99)

How You Can Walk in the Spirit. This booklet teaches Christians how to face real-life problems and disappointments in the power of the Holy Spirit and enables you to be victorious over temptation. Part of the Transferable Concept series. (64 pp., $1.99)

Now, for the first time, you can lead a fasting and prayer gathering in your small group or in your church or community. Step-by-step instructions on how to develop a leadership team and conduct the gathering. (48 pp., $4.99)

These books and booklets are available through your local Christian bookstore, mail-order catalog distributor, or NewLife Publications.

Ask us about our special quantity discounts.
Call toll-free today: (800) 235-7255, ext. 376.

Response Form

☐ Dr. Bright, I want to be one of the two million people who will join you in forty days of fasting and prayer for revival.

☐ Please send me information on quantity discounts for *The Coming Revival,* the *7 Basic Steps to Successful Fasting and Prayer,* and the *Preparing for the Coming Revival* manual and video package to give to my pastor, church, loved ones, and friends.

☐ Please inform me of other materials on how I can be filled with the Holy Spirit and be more effective in my Christian witness.

_____
NAME

_____
ADDRESS

_____
CITY

_____
STATE   ZIP
(   )
_____
PHONE

Please check the appropriate box(es) and mail this form in an envelope to:

    Bill Bright
    Campus Crusade for Christ
    P.O. Box 593684
    Orlando, FL 32859

Or send E-mail to NewLife Publications at:

    CompuServe: 74114,1206
    Internet: newlife@magicnet.net